POEMS
I WROTE
FOR YOU.

my grand gesture,

Ranhald Froulis

ISBN: 978-9976-5579-3-0

DEDICATION

I dedicate this to the one who showed me a type of love that nether my mother, my soul, nor my sister, my sweet Lutukela couldn't

I won't say your name in this one, but I have done well to spell it out loud throughout the book.

Contents

5

I didn't understand why,
why it is so easy falling....,
falling in love with you at every chance I get,
I couldn't figure it out why love felt different with you,
until I realized it hadn't been love with anybody else

SONG

she is a rose of Sharon, a lily of the valley,
like an apple tree among the trees of the forest,
is my lover among the young women,
her fruit is forever sweet to my taste,
she strengthen me when I'm faint with her love,
my head is under her left arm,
and her right arm embraces me,
I delight to sit in her shade,

Shh!!
"Do not arouse nor awaken love until it desires",
listen! Look! Here she comes,
leaping across the mountains, bounding over the hills,
gazing through the windows, peering through the lattice

"Arise my darling, my beautiful one, come with me,
you see! The winter is past, the rains are over
flowers have start to appear on the earth,
the fig trees forms their early fruit as they once did,
daisies on the fields are as white as they can be,
and the season of singing has come,
my dove let me hear your voice for your voice is sweet,
show me your face for your face is lovely",
my lover is mine and I am hers,

ROMORS

Rumors true lies
People tend to talk on what they see,
we don't ask what is real, always quick to judge,
we create our own version of an event,
and as it pass from one mouth to another ear, spreading like
cancer underneath the skin,
taking root deep in to the minds of the hearing,
and in a flash a lie becomes the truth we believe in, it
becomes a concrete contradicting story,
leading to burning of bridges,
destruction of reputations,
and limonene to sweet moments made,
only at a point when it's late,
we realize we can do too little about it,
for we have lost it all, and non gained,
what was once fine is no longer part of the set,
 Rumors poison made by tongues,
…….rumors!

I

I'm not your Mr. Right right now,
I don't know your favorite color,
I don't know what you like to eat,
I don't know how you like your tea,
I don't know what makes you angry,
………but I want to,
I want a girl like you,
trust me less, just allow me to teach you,
let me show you what you yet know,

no, I don't want your body,
I'm not in for a Marilyn Manroe,
I'm in for more than what I see,

I want your time, a fix in your schedule
darling I want to be your priority,
to be present in your prayers, in your thoughts
I want to be part of you, you part of us,
for when you walked into the room my heart was stolen,
the moment my eyes met you for the first time,
when my ears heard you sing,
 right then my heart was satisfied,
I knew you are the one meant to silence my screaming
        heart,
the end to my endless circle, my final frontier,
maybe I'm just young and stupid,
maybe I'm not thinking straight,
maybe I don't know what I'm signing up for,
maybe you are complicated than you appear,
how will I know unless I find out,
unless you let me figure it out,
just close your eyes and take a leap of faith?,

15

and I promise never to scar your precious heart,
for I was made for loving you,
and it's what I intend to do

She gave her Diamond heart,
to a guy who wanted it gold.

US

what happened to us,
I thought we were doing fine,
you had me with your smile,
I did my best to keep your smile,
I didn't do my best to keep you smiling,

how did we fall apart so fast?,
did I do something not?,
did I say something inappropriate?,
did I offend you in any way?,
I'm sorry if I did, I never knew nor intended to

like a hot shower in a cold day,
the warmth leaving the body,
is how you strayed from me,
so quick, so fast, so rapid
you didn't show me a sign,
you should have given me a hint,
you left me with a Q&A without the A,
that did a number on me,
I have never been at ease ever since,

maybe it's true "good things are over fast",
yet here I am still clinging on to the lost moments,
for in those moments I had true happiness,
they said "if you want something,
all you have to do is ask for it",
what I want is to be wanted by you,
I know "everything happens for a reason",
the reason here is my stupidity,
I sometimes go to the past to the moments I cherish,
the place I take myself to have a glance at bliss,

for my reality is not how I want it,
I go back to my class seat where you were close to me,
where you let me entertain you with my stories,
stories you knew I exaggerate, yet still listened

 I go to that school balcony,
where we watched the birds fly back to the trees,
I watch you and me watch the evening turn to night,
where you touch my soul with every touch,
always hated when you walked away,
I knew then that I needed you for everything

*H*eaven
must be less interesting
without you in it.

YOU

I just want something real,
with someone different, with you
for you are a definition of a real lady,
I know it's hard to believe me,
besides I'm just another guy,

I didn't want to make you mad,
I wanted to keep you happy,
I turned around and cried in silence,
I decided to have you from a distant,
 have you in my heart,
but keep me from your site,
had no one to talk to so I said it in my poems,
and hoped one will find it's way to you,
I built a wall and hide behind my jokes,
but lately the wall hasn't been holding up,
I mean I think of you till I sleep,

last night in my dream you made my heart race,
they say "if you love someone,
sometimes you have to let them go,
if they are yours to begin with they will be back",
I never believed it, now I do
cause darling, I did let you go
and here you are, just like they said

now I want to call you "baby" know I mean it,
I am saying "I need you" from my heart I believe it,
I am saying "I love you",
for I found love for me in an exquisite girl,
whose eyes hold my joy,
and your smile is all want,

FEAR

"fear" the enemy, "time" the thief,
the fear of rejection made me silent over the time,
always knew what to say but not how to say it,
did nothing than listen,
and I heard you found a cooler guy,
left me wishing I had said more than a couple of words,
maybe for some reason it would have made a difference,
maybe I might have been the cooler guy,
I watched……….,
watched you smile, cry, laugh, walk, sit, stand and talk
I'm sorry it's the way I handled the rush of having a crush
       on you,

I just want to look at you,
and have you look at me back,
but "love is a two way road",
sometimes both roads are busy,
sometimes just one,
I don't blame you,
we don't choose who we love,
and every year I remind myself,
"eventually I will be fine",
if I keep on saying "it is not meant to be",
a point will come that I will believe it.

GOD

I asked God for a map to a better place,
all the roads I took lead me to you,
I have lost myself in a maze of your words,
the compass for my deepest desire,
still points North to you,

so they can tell my Mom I'm careful now,
all it took is a look from your eyes,
and the silence from your lips,
to make me know without you I will be torn apart,
tell my Dad his son is an addict,
I can't do a day without you in my veins,
and I'm very far gone, too deep for rehab

I told you I will never tell you a lie,
that's why I won't promise you forever,
I yet know of tomorrow,
I'm no prophet nor messier,
but,
we can have "for all ways" if we try,

don't tell me I impress you,
that's not what I plan to do,
I want to amaze you,
show you all the best we have had,
is yet to be bested,
just stick with me, you will see

NOW

"Now" the only time we truly have,
a past we create in the present,
the time that matters in a story,
now to tell this story right,
I must begin at the right moment,
I must start at Now,

now is a meeting of two strangers,
not planned nor expected,
just the forces of nature at play,

now two are friends,
we laugh together, joke at each other
creating moments for the memory to keep,
so ignorant of tomorrow's possibilities,

now I'm stupid and an idiot,
speak so many words,
never the ones I mean you to here,

now is an end to a relationship,
without a reason not even one,
no more sweet talks nor dialogues,
death to a yet blossomed something,

now is the middle of the story,
we only express "hi" from a distance,
smiles, nodding heads, and a waving hand
a conversation ends without a word said,

now we talk and I feel alive again,
time to time we meet and say things,
filled with words to say and no way to speak,
Yet I'm trying to stay connected,
straggling to get your attention,

and finally NOW,
now I'm certain that I love you,
I wish so hard to fill you in,
but I don't know where to start ,

and Now I don't want to upset you,
I don't want to Frown your face,
I don't want my vibe to kill your mood,
 for "now!" is the only moment I have with you.

All I want
For my birthday
is you and a long life
that doesn't come with
punctuation marks

I VOW

with this ring, I vow to always be the left side of your right,
always be your push up the hill and your shade in the
desert,
when you are angry and screaming words that hurt, that
break me,
I know you won't mean any, so I won't go too far away,
I vow to make you feel safe from harm in the shelter of my
arms,
I vow to hold your waist and gaze into your eyes as I do the
stars,
I will tell you how beautiful you are to my eyes when you
feel insecure,
if rumors gets too loud, I vow to whisper things that will
make you smile
in the evening at the coast as the sun sets beyond the
horizon,
I will have your head on my shoulders as we watch ocean
water form waves,
and as the winds gets colder, I am the coat that keeps your
skin warm
I am the pillow to your slumber, and if nightmares keeps
you awake
my heart is your sandman throughout the darkest night,
you are imperfect and the best version of me,
and I wouldn't have it any other way

GRASS

what do you do when the one you love,
doesn't know how you feel,

I wish you knew I want you,
it's a secret I try to hide,
but you are here in my heart,
deep down in my soul I know,
you are the one I have been waiting for,
even though I never been positive,
somehow I am sure this is how it feels to be in love,
for every time my eyes meet yours,
I feel bliss and awe to my knees,

maybe the grass is greener on the other side,
maybe it's not, I don't know
I never turned the leaf,
I was afraid to find out,
afraid you might leave while I still want this,
I don't want you to turn around and walk away,
it will crush me to dust,
I want you to stay,
reason why I kept it a secret,
admire you from a distance,
for what's the point of admitting,
if all it's going to cause is pain.

SHE!

she is a bird with a broken wing,
she can't fly, so she just cry a song,
she got bent beyond her breaking point,
yet she smiles to hide the pain in her eyes,
she wants love but she is afraid,
she has issues, she don't want to trust you,
she has proved "disappointment comes from those you love",
she had her heart broken, ripped from her chest,
now she pushes away everything close enough to affection,
for she expects to be left in the end, so push is now a reflex

you can try, you can bend your back backwards ten times,
and still won't dazzle her when you are done performing,
she is happier alone, in being single she is happiest,
it's not that she don't care, she just don't want to bother

Chéri

Well very one knows chéri,

but not the way I do, you see!,
she don't need makeup to be beautiful, God was in no rush,
she has a smile on her face that defines my meaning of life,
she has the ugliest laughter and she knows it, yet still finds
      everything funny
I'm not sure why she punches when she laugh it's a habit I
      think,
she don't have that neck turning figure,
but I'm turned by her simple curves when she moves,
she never dress to impress, but I'm impressed with how
      she dresses
when you don't see how sexy the way she flicks her hair
      back her shoulder,
it's because you are not paying attention to the details in
      the movements,
watch how she leans back as she positions her hand under
      her hair,
watch the way her lips are unclosed and her eyes half open
      as she toss her hair to the back,
watch how she apply that final touch with her figure cross
      her fore head,
but you don't see that because you are just looking,

she is no angel, she is imperfect
her eyes rain tears, she has her fears
she has secrets and she has regrets,
she has skeletons in her closet with walls inside a wall to
      keep it locked,
way to her body is through her heart that no one has the
      keys to,
You see she has less trust on how is not her,
and if I wasn't so ugly,
she would probably give me a chance

*R*unning home to you,
Falling right into your arms,
is all I want to do

CARDS

never have I ever been good at cards,
I have never known what to throw down,
my actions always betray the secrets in my lies,
mixed signals my eyes on you,
you look at me and look away when I notice,
I look at you and pretend I'm not staring,
we lock eyes at we and we smile before we break,
I say "hi" then nothing comes out,
you bite that tongue when you've something to say,
but my tears are a heart break away,
you shake my hand and walk away,
I watch you go, you don't look back
I see you disappear at a corner,
my heart crakes a new crake,

though I have loved you for a thousand years,
you are still known for loving yourself,
so I pin my earphones and drown myself,
drift away in Ed Sheraan's lyrics,
fantasize in "how would you feel",
or maybe "little bird" will encourage me to "dive",
I imagine us in "wake me up" in "perfect",

and I wish I didn't love you this much,
but I do,
I have come to the edge and jumped over the ledge,
I'm shooting for great,
Good ain't great, you are great,

CRUSH

Hey it's your long term crush,
I know you don't know me,
but you have been living in my heart for aeons,
I fell in love with you in one moment,
and I haven't stopped ever since,
but that part you won't know,
for from what I heard,
you hate relations and I can't handle rejection,
our waters wasn't meant to mix,
so I bite my tongue and seal my lips,
for the words "I love you" will chess you away,
I can't have you walk away,
I don't want you to walk away,

It's easier to fantasize,
easier to imagine you for mine,
hard to fathom you for me,
the things I could not say out loud,
I found a place to write them down,
hoped they will find their way to you,

you show me you don't need me,
your system to keep me out is perfect,
as perfect as your lips when you smile,
the combination of your half closed eyes
and a pinch of teeth shown,
is just enough to show perfection.

I WISH

every time I see a shooting star,
I make a wish,
I wish to forever be the ignition of your love,
the spark that lits your desire,
I wish to forever live in your heart,
stay there till your eyes knows my secretes,
till your blood runs my name,
till thoughts of me dominate your mind,

I wish to be there when you wake up,
where I can ask you how you slept,
so you can tell me about your dreams,
I wish to be there when you cook,
so I can taste your every meal,
I wish to be the only one who holds you tight,
have you close to me in every passing minute,
I wish to miss you every second of the day,
so that I remember how much I need you,
I wish to hold your head up by the neck,
kiss your lips till we run out of breath,
I wish to always make you smile,
I wish to never wipe tears from your face,
rather be the shoulder you cry your pain away,
I wish to be your one and only, forever and for always

STORY

I would like to tell you a story,
and like any romantic story,
this one starts with the ears,

before I met you I heard whispers,
I knew your name way before I saw you,
for your reputation precedes you,
you beauty was all all talked about,
and the moment I laid my eyes on you,
I knew then that words can't do you justice,

as my eyes had their satisfaction,
my mind drew a conclusion,
yes I have feelings for you,
and I am afraid of that,
you in my life is what I want most,
but telling you how I really feel meant two things,
losing it all, or having it all,
I am known for not taking huge risks,
decided to call you my friend,
zoned myself in the friendzone,
thought that way I will keep us close,
maybe my silence is what drove you away, or
maybe you knew of my feelings but you didn't feel the
        same way,
either way we created a wall between us

people talk, relations grow, you stopped

and I was hurt by that, I got lost
I tried the lunatic living but it was not for me,
I did my name, I "ran" as fast as I could,
but when I stopped all I saw was you,

 Yo tengo "mi alma", yo tengo "mi vida",
all I'm asking is for you to give me "my heart",
and as romantic story's happily ever after,
this one's end is all upon you,
I could fall or we could fly depending on the words you say

*O*ne *t*ime when you were next to me,
under the night sky full of stars,
I swear the moon seemed brighter in your eyes

RIGHT NOW?

Where are you right now?,
are you some where cold?,
is you some place warm?,
are you laughing from a joke?,
or are you forcing a smile?,
are you holding you pillow tightly close to your skin?,
are you wishing to have me by your side?,
are your nights long and lonely like mine?,
are you gazing at the sky?,
do you see the twinkle in the stars?,
did you talk to the moon last night?,
I think I heard her whisper my name!,
did you send this wind a kiss?,
I felt a smooch when it blew me by,
Where are you right now?,
for I am not where you are and it hurts

DON'T

"don't force things to happen,
some weren't meant to be"
I need to keep that in mind,
I know you are way out of my league,
practically a different species,
but yet I still hope for something,
for nothing is all I have,
a man's heart is strong but easy to break,
small things like one sided dialogues,
unanswered or ignored phone calls,
such tiny things maybe nothing to one,
to another, they are enough to crush a soul

maybe you are doing it on purpose,
please don't toy with my emotions,
it's torment in every sixty seconds of sixty minutes,
torturous in every twenty four hours of seven days,
so if you don't want me the same way,
better lay it on me straight, no games
it's not fine but Ok,

I know you ain't leaving my heart,
so I will find a way to numb my feels,
I will go back behind the sidelines,
find my special seat and keep watching,
I will find that silent corner and make my noise,
find a pen and paper to scream my feelings,

just promise to do that gently,
just go easy and slow, give me room to breath
allow me to reminisce on the sweet memories of us,
give me the leisure of adjusting to the fact,
don't stake me to the heart and watch me burn,
give me a chance to enjoy the last sun set,

yet again I am glad,
for I got to feel how it really feels
to truly love the most exquisite girl
ever to be seen by my eyes to the extent
I am afraid of both
yes and no from a proposal,
how loco is that???,
but………,
"don't force things to happen!"

Nothing
is ever more
exquisite
when you smile

I KNOW

I don't know what this is
maybe it's a crush,
maybe it's love,
maybe it's an obsession,
maybe it's an infatuation,
I don't know what this is,

all I know is I have had these feelings for years,
I know that every time I see of you I get nervous,
I sleep thinking of green lights I didn't notice,
I know that I daydream of what might be,
I know that every time I see you I feel awe,
I know that when you leave so goes my joy,
I know that I want you all the time,
I know that we are always more in my dreams,
I think you are pushing me away now,
or you are testing my persistence,
I know that I don't know how you truly feel about me,
I know that I will break if you love me in a different way,
I know that I won't be surprised if you don't feel the same,
I know that you make me believe in a tomorrow,
and I know that I will love you to the grave,
I know that you think I'm lying,
I know that I'm not
I know that I die,
I know that you don't care.

HE SAID

He said
"we will start hearing rumors about us,
something that will make no sense,
that you were caught kissing somebody,
and I'm sleeping with someone else,
Yes, they may sound bit crazy,
I know you know it isn't true,
and before we start acting monkey,
throwing all glass to wall,
making me high five your face,
and you hitting my clutch,
sometimes they might send you pictures,
which I'm with other girls,
I know you'll be quick to judge me,
I'm not saying that you are wrong,
I know it isn't bad, but annoying,
when you start asking the questions
those Who, When, Where, Why
with killer in your eyes and tears down you chicks,
baby it's alright to be mad and doubtful,
I know there is no true love without jealousy,
but before things escalate,
can we hold hands,
and let our lips hit reset,
to that lovebird morning sunshine,
where it's just us, and
everything is alright"

BROKEN

heartbroken, and rejected
the pain is extreme,
by that I have been so scared to be attached again,
I have this fear that any person I start to like,
will go on and break my heart,
and that was the beginning of being lonely,
all because I was hurt once,
then you came along,
it was your smile where the trouble started,
the smile worth a thousand words,

maybe we are all the same,
maybe we are not,
maybe you are the next mistake,
or maybe I'm your charming,
either way I'm not in it for a good time,
for I can't fall for more than one,
I dive when I do,
I only make a promise I can keep,
I'm in it for the long time,
next to my dreams,
I have never been so sure in my life,
you are the reason my heart still beats,
I don't know if you believe me,
I don't know if you can,
what I know is you have a story,

maybe a guy disappointed you once,
maybe your hero took you heart and broke your trust,
maybe it's the reason you always smile,
you are trying to hide the scars he left behind,
maybe every time your heart skips a beat,
you turn around, you run so fast that the flash can't catch
        you,
but I don't know your story,

I hope to know your story,
I promise to give a new story,

Just wish things were different,
wish you were with me,
just wish I was with you,
I wish you wished the same too,
I wish wishes came true

CHANCE

it's complicated,
did it once before, didn't want to do it again,
never been known to take extreme risks,
but you are always sweet and happy,
you feel me with awe in everything,
so I'm taking a chance,
yes there is a possibility that I will hurt me,
and I will be left wishing I never knew the truth,
wishing I stayed in the dark,
but there is also a chance I will find joy,
an element to suppress my loneliness,
there is a chance that you are waiting for me to start,
there is a chance you feel the way I do,
sorry if I took a chance at love,
diving in to a world I know nothing about,
hopping together we will understand it,
Would you take this chance with me?,

A MIRACLE

a miracle, turning silk into Gold,
your father a man you so despise,
upon all the people he met,
one of them is your mother,
the woman you love so dearly,
and with all that happened,
the before and after mistakes, the chaos all of each,
they all lead to the creation of you,
one perfect organism that no one can get enough of,
all the pain and tears,
led to the forgery of what you are this very moment,
a lady with a twenty four hours smile to die for,
a darling to cherish forever and hold too close,
one so delicate and unique to be mishandled,
it's like turning silk into Gold,
"a miracle"

DEAR YOU

Dear you,
I know I'm a fool,
maybe I'm coming on too strong,
I know I have waited too long,
you tell me if I'm playing my cards wrong,

I wish I had said this sooner,
but I'm with fear of rejection,
the heart and the head, a delicate combination
my heart told me to let it out,
my head told me to keep it in,

do I sleep with you in my mind?
YES!
do I rehearse how to tell you about my dreams?
only every day,
do I tell myself today is the day?
NO!.....
because I don't have the guts for it,
I always see how it's going to go,
I see me walk on to you,
I see you walk away from me,
I see me in the corner alone,
also I see you smile and hold my hand,
then fear drives my fight away,

I know I can't give you much,
you already have enough,
what I can give is a promise,
for I jumped with thousands of rocks in your lake,
I hope royalty is what you need,

please don't hate me for writing the truth,
no, I would never lie to you,
but it's not fine to lose you,
I do love you, I do want your love,
I thought it will pass if I let go,
and with time it will fade away,
I turned to poetry as an escape from you,
it turned to be a secrete place where we meet,

I'm only human,
don't blame me for loving you,
if you were me you would love you too,
I'm sorry for the honesty,
but I have to get this off my chest,
I have to let you know you are the
    "reina de mi corazón".

*L*ove
is merely
a strong enough
Word
if I'm to describe
the way I feel about you

SHE DON'T

She don't talk much,
she stays quite and listens,
but when she speaks even
the deaf hear and the dead wake

She don't look much,
she press her eyes shut,
but when she reveals them,
the whole world stops to stare

She don't touch much
she keeps her skin to herself
but when she does
cactus turns daises

She don't walk much,
she vault her feelings within,
but when she does, she can't control it,
she dives in head first

She don't smile much,
she locks that move by chains,
but when she does, it has the cure
and your problem cease to exist

She don't like friends much,
she sticks her relationship at heart,
she hates the betrayal and hypocrisy,
she would rather live alone and lonely

She don't cry much,
She has nothing to make that,
but when she does, it's of a great cause,
the tears are no other than joy

she don't dance much,
she keeps her style from her thighs,
but when she does all you will see is………..

Under my breath,
I will shout your name
after I scream "I LOVE YOU!"

SOMEONE

Love is such a dreadful bond,
if you have it, you keep it,
get a hold on it,
for it is something special,
those who lost it,
when they see it, the feel it,
the tender, the texture,
it makes you want to have someone,

 Someone to touch in a different way,
someone to kiss and make it ok,
someone to love sick away,
someone to miss when you are apart,
someone to cause butterflies in your gut,
someone to comfort you when you are lonely,
a shoulder to cry on, arms to hold tight,
someone to see you as one in a million,
someone to fill the vacuum of the heart,
someone to quench your desire,
someone to be one for the keeping

LAST NIGHT

Last night I had a dream,
in that dream I dreamt about you and I,

in this world of my imagination,
you called me honey when I called you darling,
you woke me up with a kiss in the mornings,
you needed no pillow, my chest is comfy you said

we laughed all the time,
you blushed most of the time,
your perfect smile in the dialogues,
the way you looked at me as you listened,
how you move your lips when you replied,

It was magic when your skin touched mine,
made my blood boil and goose bumps all over,
for every touch from your palm was sensational,
seeing the lover in your words!,
the keeper in your actions!,
darling I fell in love with you all over again,
made me feel beyond blessed,

then I woke up you weren't there,
I died a little, looked at of you
and the living part smiled

WITH YOU

I want to explore places with you,
create the best memories out of moments,
enjoy life with everything that comes with it,
I want to do every little thing
with you,

I want to see the sun under the grey clouds,
watch the rain as it falls down from the sky,
feel a drop after a drop on our skin,
shiver from cold then cuddle for warmth
with you

I want to stay and blossom in your love,
break and scatter in your doubts,
pick up the large pieces and give them to you,
smoothen the rough edges of us,
with you

I want to tell you how beautiful you are before your
makeup,
show you how you steal the attention in the crowd,
how you voice settles disputes in my head,
how I find myself in a state of bliss when I'm
with you

I want to start at alpha and watch omega pass us by,
I want to dive head first to your rocky bottomed lake,
find out the story after "happily ever after"
with you

I want to only speak the truth with no secrets,
use my heart while it's still beating,
cause darling when you are right next to me,
there is no other place I would rather be,
my house is home, only if in it I'm
with you

I want to explore places, feel the rain,
break my heart, feel bliss,
find love, have something to loose
find it all in you,
Darling only with you

God gave us ice cream,
ice cream is great,
you are the best thing
since ice cream

THE TIMES I SAW HER

The first time I saw her,
she passed me by,
like a shooting star does to the sky,
made me wish she would be mine

The second time I saw her,
her face had a smile,
and her voice sounded "hey!"
Suddenly I fell in love with that

The third time I saw her,
she saw me, see her,
for seconds we stared at each other,
we both smiled and looked away

The fourth time I saw her,
my eyes met hers,
a certain chill was born in me,
and my heart went to a rabbit race

The fifth time I saw her,
her lips called my name
and I said "hi"
right then I knew she was the one

The sixth time I saw her,
my hands touched hers,
 a cold sweat run down my spine,
and my heart skipped a beat

The seventh time I saw her,
she was sitting on my favorite seat,
the dilemma in my heart
grew intense tenfold

The eighth time I saw her
I couldn't keep what I felt within,
I told her the truth, so to be free,
she blushed and walked away from me

The ninth time I saw her,
she saw me from a distance,
like similar magnets she moved,
my mind felt sorry for my heart

The tenth time I saw her,
she came to me,
unexpectedly tapped my shoulder,
slowly moved to my ear and said "I'm in"

The eleventh time I saw her,
while next to me she said,
" hope my heart is safe with you"
I said, "like a princess in a castle"

The twelfth time I saw her,
it was our first date, on her birthday,
the day was covered with laughter and smiles
and under the black sky we had our first kiss

The thirteenth time I saw her,
she gave me the taste of her lips,
she held my hands and said,
"I pray for this to our seventy's"

The fourteenth time I saw her,
it was at the church,
I fixed a ring on it and loudly said,
"TILL DEATH DO US APART!"

The fifteenth time I saw her,
She had a short night dress on,
lights were off, only candles burnt romance,
we made the bed sing and the sheets scream!,

The sixteenth time I saw her,
she had a big belly, twins to be precise,

The seventeenth time I saw her,
I held her by the waist and pulled her close,
kissed her for a minute or two,
and told her "we made it to our seventy's"

The eighteenth time I saw her,
her body was too weak
to even move her lips

The last time I saw her,
She was lying on her bed,
with oxygen and food pipes in her
she said "I love you" with a smile and a tear
then her heart beats went silent.

WEAKEST

you fisherman you,
a worm to fish you had me fooled,
your wits and dos lured me to your hook,
your siren song sweet to my ears tricked me,
I can't shake off this feeling,
this bliss when you are here,
the lust when you not near,
I just want to be with you,
I hate to admit that I'm falling for you,
but I am just a young boy trying to be loved!,
eager to make you love me back,
So go ahead and break my heart again,
leave me wondering why the hell I let you in,
is it because I love you more than I should?,
but yet again great castles demise from within,
guess you had me at my weakest,

A LETTER TO MY LOVER

Hey!,
did I tell you how beautiful you seem to me
when you show me your smile with those ocean eyes,
how you say "hey" I your morning voice,

tell who ever is coming that I am staying
show them the way out, for I ain´t leaving,
´cause you have taken my heart for you,
and I think I will give up my soul too,

you know it breaks my heart when you leave,
it always makes me sad and wonder
¨to where are you going?..., you are home!¨,

I want to keep you close,
kiss you, hold you and never let go,
´cause we only live once and I don't want to risk it,
yesterday won't be back as tomorrow is non but a dream,
so let´s live today like it´s our last,

please darling,
keep me swimming in this pool of your love,
teach me to paddle in this stream of your affection,
and when we hear thunder made by angry Thor,
as the waves hits our ark, shaking us to our core
hold my hand through the strange tides,
and I promise the white dove will fly back to us,

hey!, Good morning,

Ps,
I Love You.

93

MY LOVE

you are wearing that cologne I like,
those eyes lashes, and shadow eyes!,

you look so beautiful in that dress,
I see your hair, I love your hair like that,
I love how you wear that smile on your lips,
the way they move to the sides of your face,
it's the final touch to a perfect date,
and if this is to be the last thing I see,
I thank God that it's you that it is,

you look so wonderful in this light!,
how you steal the spotlight when we walk in,
everybody is paying attention,
close to see what they are missing,
I am not a religious man, but
I thank God every day for giving me you,

we are always surrounded,
surrounded with all of these people,
people with mouths that talk too much,
but you always have that looks in your eyes,
that tells me there is nothing and no one else but us,
with it everything fades away as you take a breath,

breathing ever so slightly on my chest,
as we dance in silhouette to your song,
and if this is to be the last thing I do,
I would want no other than it to be with you,

for as you are here now, right next to me,
I know now I never truly knew how a heart beats,
and I just want to tell you I love you,
then show you how much I mean when say it,

'cause from the moment I knew you, Shon
you are all I knew I will ever need

*O*n this hill I will build my church,
In your head I will build my respect,
Upon your heart I will build my trust

THREE WORDS

sometimes you just don't have a choice,
you can't help but think of someone,
think of their lips when they smile,
you can't help but want them in your arms,
desire to get more than what they give,
you see a whole life with them,
yet fail it see it all the same,

three words,
three words on the tip of my tongue,
maybe they were all you wanted to hear,
darling fear got the best of me,
the fear of you saying "no",
more the fear of you saying "yes",
the fear that I don't deserve you,

I can't promise not to hurt you,
I'm only human, I ain't perfect
but I will do my best to do it less,
and when your love starts to fade,
I will give you a reason to stay,
for what value is my life,
if you are not in it.

WHEN I LOVE YOU

I want you to know how happy you make me feel,
even though at times it is painful,
I want you to know I love every part of it,
I don't know if what we had was love,
but if it wasn't I wonder what love feels like,

I want you to know that I'm sorry if I pushed you away,
I never meant to, what I meant was to bring you closer,
and if, even for a moment I was ever like home to you,
then you must have felt safe in the presence of me,
and I hope to be your safe heaven one more time,

I want you to know this most of all,
in your company I am at my most happiest,
I want you to be happier, and if it has to be,
even if every nerve of mine might not like it,
I want someone else to know the worth of your smile,
to have the chemicals burst as I do when I see you,
to feel the same way you make me feel,
when I love you.

MY REASON WHY

you are my reason why,
the one reason why!,
the one I want to wake up to see,
reason I sleep just to be with you in my dreams,
the one reason why my pen hits the paper,
you are the one reason I bed early but sleep late,

my heart beats for a purpose,
you are the reason it beats for a reason,
The one reason why!,
why I run in circles for I ignore the way out,

I wish I could trade hearts with you,
so you can know how I really feel for you,
I don't have a forever to promise you,
most I can give you is a best moment,
and it's yours if you take it.

WHAT ARE WE?

What are we?
are we a boy and a girl?, or a boy with a girl?,
are we behind the scene?, or we on screen?,

what is happening?,
what is going on?,
what are we doing?,
who are we fooling?,

are we something serious?,
are we something legit?,
what they say, what they see
it's confusing, but so are we,

are we just mates?,
are we setting for the next phase?,
are we trying to add a word to "friend"?,

tell me what page you are in?,
I want to know if the same book we are reading,
for what we are portraying,
 isn't what we are doing

where are we now?,
where are we going?,
please give me a reason
why on I should be holding

what is this?,
what are we creating?,
I don't understand, what's our intention
so please tell me "what are we?"

IF I WAS AN ARTIST

if I was an artist,
your face would be the core source of my muse,
I would wake up in the middle of the night and when you
wake up......,
my fingers will be orange, nails filled with colors of our
sheets,
and next to me a new painting of you sound asleep,

my portraits would express the sweet type of mean that you
portray through your actions,
my walls would bare new graffiti of your name over the old
graffiti of your name,
for I would always try to find new ways to spell it out,
my studio would scatter with unfinished sculptures of your
body
cause I will never get details in your curves right

If I was an artist,
you would be the centre of my poetry,
I would describe your mesmerizing beauty in a thousand
words,
and still have more to say at the end of a page,
I would kiss you, hold you, fight and make up in every
stanza,
I would get you to sleep at the comma and wake you up at
the full stop,
I would describe how you snore in my rhymes, and how
you drool through the rhythm,

if I was an artist,
I would always get high on your smile,
your eyes would take me to places of bliss and awe,
I would snort your skin till I'm addicted to your scent
and as any addict when I relapse till I OD,
my rehab would be right between your arms,

I'm not an artist,
but if I was!!......,
my art would be about you....!,
in every paint, in every portrait, in every poem,
any form would show how imperfectly perfect you are to
        my eyes,
"every art is made for only one person"
darling mine.............
would be for you.

*M*oment that I saw you it was clear to see,
my right side looks better when I'm on your left,

IF EYES COULD SPEAK

if eyes could speak,
then my lips would have it easy,
I wouldn't have to worry on what to say,

if my eyes could speak
they would tell you all that I want to say out straight,
they would tell you how you make me speechless,
how your glance gets me breathless,
they would show you how loud my heart screams your
         name,
they would tell you that your scent fills my lungs,
they would explain why I become jealous when others get
         your attention,
they would tell you how I wish to be the solution to your
         problems,

if eyes could speak,
they would say how you numb my pain,
how you change my awful day,

if eyes could speak,
I would need not time to waste,
I would need not to wait for the right moment,
I would have no hesitation or second thoughts,

if my eyes could speak,
I would need not to talk,
I would look you in the eyes,
for one look would say everything,
just one glance would say it all,

IT'S

it's not that she don't love you,
she's just fed up of the lies and misconceptions,

if you listen to her side of the story you will understand,

she knows a breaking heart,
she is no stranger to the feeling,
to her you are just another guy,

she gave her precious heart to the worthless bastards,
she misplaced her trust and paid a heavy price for it,
so forgive her if she ignores you,
you are not the first to tell her "I Love You",

she roles her eyes at every couple,
her mind is filled with void,
for the man she once loved,
lied to her face with a smile,
promised her ALWAYS, never said FOREVER,

it's not that she feels herself,
it's not that you are not her type,
it's not that she doesn't care how you feel,
she has no time for a guy,
a relationship is not her main focus,
she is nursing her heart to health,
forgive her if she is selfish,
but she is not sorry if she is

ORANGE

I will tell you what orange is,
orange is never sweet unless it´s orange,
orange is worst for juice, but a sweet as fruit,
orange has limonene in it´s peel that makes you cry,
 Orange-

orange is always on her phone but has a late reply,
orange is full of excuses, you can't get her to stay,
she always has a place to go, she always has a thing to do if
you ask her to come,

Orange, is shy, she walks fast as if she is running from
everything,
Orange, has the ugliest laugh and laughs loud,
orange hits you when she laughs and she says sorry,
Orange, does not change her nail polish until they ware out,
orange has baggy eyes and a long forehead,
when she has not done her hair, Orange looks like a midget
in a tarban,
Orange is a heaven angel with the devil's pride,
orange can make you feel worthless with her sarcasm,

orange cries, but you will always see her smile,
orange has mistakes and orange has regrets,
Orange is flawed, she is not perfect

but Orange "I LOVE YOU!"

*E*very love poem I write,
there is a piece of you in it

•

dear eyes,
there is a lot to see but she is our only amusement
dear feet,
you always cover miles but her is our destination
dear hands,
I know you are clumsy please don't drop her heart
dear heart,
you are new here don't go wondering on your own
dear lips,
you tend to say a lot but be careful when you speak
dear ears,
please listen when she speaks always pay attention
dear brain,
know your place you are not my therapist
dear you,
I give you all that I have I hope that it is enough

Ranhald